Laying Roots: Poems on Grief and Healing

Memere
There is one thing that every Spiller has in common: resiliency. We get through the hard times together and come out stronger. Thank you for your love and support through it all.
XOXO
Amanda

poems on grief and healing

LAYING ROOTS

Written by
Amanda Spiller

Illustrated by
Jackie Zintel

Laying Roots: Poems on Grief and Healing.
Copyright © 2022 by Amanda Spiller.
All rights reserved. Printed in the United States of America. No part of this book may be used or reproduced in any manner without written permission except in the case of brief quotations embodied in critical articles and reviews. For information, email info@amandaspiller.com

Edited by Brennan DeFrisco and Sara Shopkow
Illustrated by Jackie Zintel
Designed by Marisa Randles

ISBN 979-8-9865160-1-1

FIRST EDITION

To connect with the author, email amanda@amandaspiller.com

10 9 8 7 6 5 4 3 2 1

To the people who help us lay roots.

Dear friend,

This is going to be hard, at times.

If the poems from *Root Rot* start weighing on your heartspace, mix in poems from *Root Sprout* and *Root System* to lift the weight.

You can also read the book backward so when the hard poems come, you know there's light at the end of the tunnel.

We can heal.

Love,
Amanda

TABLE of CONTENTS

Root Rot — 1
Motherless Day — 5
Rain Is for the Dead and the Grieving — 6
What Tiny Fingers Hold, Easter 2002 — 7
Dear Mom — 8
Haze — 9
When Sadness Creeps In — 12
I Wish Someone Loved Me — 13
Far Away From Home — 14
Grief Season — 15
Uprooted — 16

Root Sprout — 19
I Named My Honda Rhonda — 22
Rebloom — 24
You Are Not Alone — 26
What to Remember on Hard Days — 28
Don't Be Afraid of Your Silence — 29
A Moose Told Me Not to Worry — 30
What To Do With Overwhelm — 32
Something Is Changing Within Me — 33
Woman in the Moonlight — 34

Root System — 37
Woman in the Moonlight II — 40
You Will Know What You Lived For — 42
Slanted Light — 43
My Backyard in the Bay (I'm not okay) — 44
You Can Enjoy the View — 46
Laying Roots — 47

The Healing Process	48
Growing a Garden	49
Dead Sunflower Sprouts	50
What You Can Do With Your Darkness	52
About the Author	54
About the Illustrator	55
Gratitude	56
Acknowledgements	57

ROOT ROT

Disease and lack of oxygen cause the plant's roots to decay, often characterized by the yellowing or wilting of leaves.

Unable to take in the oxygen, water, and nutrients needed for growth, the plant stops blooming and dies.

Mom's a rooter, so she ends up in the ground first. Before she dies, she tries to make a perfect life: the husband, the kids, the big backyard and picket fence.

When Dad realizes he'll never fit inside her idea of perfect, he leaves. This is the first time I see a family crack in half. I'm eight and I cry in math class. Numbers hurt. They never fully explain why five minus one means dinners without Dad.

Dad's a rooter, too, so he and my stepmom buy a big, four-bedroom house and fill it. Her paintings go up on the walls and a couch from Goodwill sprouts up across from a new, supersized TV. They splurge on a seashell-white one for the family room that hugs the woodfire stove. It's so soft and elegant I wonder how on earth they'll keep it from getting stained. Death is messy.

My attitude pierces the façade of normalcy. I oscillate between vitriol and silence. My stepmom works to keep the chaos at bay, fluttering about in fits of repair: removing shoes from the entryway, putting a folded pillar of laundry on each of our beds, calming us down from ourselves. By the time Dad comes home from work, dinner simmers on the stovetop. The table's set and illuminated in a soft chandelier glow.

Anyone can get used to a cadence of care. We eat meals that take hours to make. She moderates our TV intake. We argue and then remake.

I learn how an empty heart can fill with time spent on soft couches.

That version of family fissured when my stepmom went to jail. Our combined heartbreak spilled out from the lapse of her containment. Boxes, dishes, and grief piled high. It was an unspoken encroachment; every room became cluttered and dejected.

Now, I come home from college and spend my days cleaning. I search for the seats of the seashell couch, now spotted brown and covered in waves of laundry, cat divots under each window. I cradle neat clumps of cat vomit to the trash can. I blaze my way to the couch's cloth seats, doing loads and loads of laundry until I find them again.

In the kitchen, I wash days of dishes and dig my way to dilapidated tiles. Some are unattached from the wood below. I never find the right configuration or sticky-enough glue to reattach the missing pieces.

The house is a losing battle, so I carve my space in the attic. I lay down a tattered rug and put a mattress on top, along with a freshly painted desk, some plastic shelving from Lowe's, and an entertainment-system-turned-bedside table, adorned with a lamp for soft-glowing when the sun disappears from its perch.

It has been a series of unfortunate events.

I can't stay, not given the steady undoing of this house. I can't find myself within its metastasis, a shattered life that dreamt of being something else.

I consolidate everything I own into four small boxes. I set off with what I need on my back.

Motherless Day

The springtime florals are here
I drive extra slow past medians of poppies
to catch a glance of their dancing heads
nodding yes with their seasonal juices
challenging the blues with orange's nuisance

The springtime florals are here
I walk extra slow down Berkeley sidewalks
looking up at flowering shrubs
paying close attention
they told me I might find you here
or in a breeze
and although I haven't yet
I still look just in case

You aren't here
but the springtime florals are
blithely they go about it
the bobbing, the growing, the being
they show us how to soak in sun
without questioning how it's meant to help us
and how to feel life and death
in more ways than one

I came to Point Richmond
every piece of sidewalk was parallel-parked
we came here to catch the weekend before it
slipped out Sunday's door
we came here to connect with our mothers
or at least with the waves they left behind
the first roll of ice over toes will always be
a welcome surprise

The ocean has its ways
like the poppies
of joining us in the haze
as sun reflects off its open face we remember:
flowers aren't the only wonders of color
is not the sun a poppy in the sky?
tears aren't the only drops of liquid salt

Here the pebbles know it well
as waves roll down their cheeks
they settle in for the ride
and as saltwater inches closer to my feet
I wonder if the next time we meet we'll sit side by side
looking out over the vast blue
if so, I'll thank the   poppies and the ocean
for bringing me   closer to you

Rain Is For the Dead and Grieving

Rain is for the dead and the grieving
those who do not feel in words
but in sound and cadence
it is their earthbound conversation
the patter on the roof is
a limbic melody
that slows and quickens
the trees humbly bow
the soil, wettened, expresses
its nutrients and gratitude
the space in between each droplet
invites you to let go
that is rain's only urgency, to let go
there is tranquility in its release
the clouds promise that
while the world is cold, wet, and exposed
the cascade will catch your heartache
weigh it to the ground
wash its excess
out to sea

What Tiny Fingers Hold, Easter 2002

An egg!
Mom's eyes
rush through excited
I grip the egg tighter
stepdad bangs
in the kitchen
where on TV
families smile
over casseroles
and pass the salt
in ours we decompress
the past assault
Mom cocks her pocket
lights up a death rocket
in her eyes
glossed over
I see myself
shrouded in doubt
and smooth my face
furrows erased
egg spills
from my fingers
too small to hold it all
shell shrapnel
slices skin
slender lines of blood
bubble up
I shove it in my pocket
there's nothing
to see here

Dear Mom

Your husband is time
counted in symptoms
four stages too severe

> I find him in places he never was
> in the indignant arms of angry men
> in the men I fuck

You are a martyr
a list of dos and don'ts
dead so I can live

> I find you in places you never were
> in the fibers of a Walmart T-shirt
> in the first silk-scoop of Jif peanut butter

I am a lackluster atheist
bleeding without her creator
a sister; incapable mother

> I find myself in places we never were
> in a taqueria between two city streets
> in a better life

Haze

I woke up with a haze in my head
this happens after death
when her body went limp there was one thing to do
kissed her head, packed my bag and all the pictures, too

I drove down 95
left it all behind
drove her right into
a tiny corner of my mind

An unfamiliar fate greeted me at the door
a family I barely knew and had no feelings for
even with their love, I couldn't find what I had lost
my soul was steeped, six feet deep, in an eternal frost

I drove down 95
left it all behind
drove her right into
a tiny corner of my mind

When heaven sang her in, almost took my breath for good
my harmonies rang trite, my world turned black and white
yet in knowing her so well, there's a gift I'll always hold
I find her in the breeze and in the women just as bold

When Sadness Creeps In

It's not easy to stay
in this city
in this room
on this page
I have a three-month shelf life
change is my only constant
new places
new faces
new situations
a shell of myself did everything
I love this weekend
she biked
she danced
she ate buttermilk pancakes
she cuddled my boyfriend
but when she laughs I don't feel it in my belly
when she's hungry I don't want to eat
blank eyes almost give her away
microwave worries pop in her brain
I think this is why it's easier to run
to move instead of coming undone
when she stops it feels like
the sadness
has won

I Wish Someone Loved Me

I wish someone loved me
could look into the orbs of my eyes
and see sunsets
could see something
I don't

Far Away From Home

The breeze anticipates snow
crisp like a McIntosh
water bathes stones
too cold to touch

I wish I could dip and flip
like the chickadee
symbiotic with wind
dive without smashing my head

Steam from my canteen
curls into a question
how can a place that's not New England
carry longing in the air?

Pine needles coat the frigid ground
resisting the dying autumn and my question
is a friend still a friend
if you don't talk to them anymore?

Grief Season

noun /ˌgrēf ˈsēzən/

Definition of *grief season*:
the period of the year marked by a past loss that is re-lived by your mind, body, and spirit, resulting in profound lethargy and sadness

Examples of *grief season* in a sentence:
// My energy is low because I started my grief season.
// Grief season is like winter for the soul. Let yourself move slower. Trust that spring will come to thaw your sadness.
// What can you do to honor your grief season?

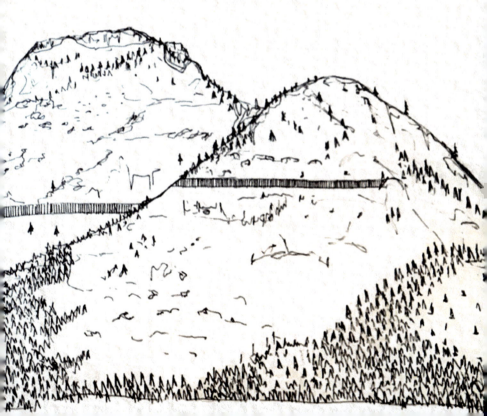

Uprooted

I'm used to the feeling of packing up and moving on. I know exactly what I have and how to fit it into my suitcase. I don't waste time or space. I fold and roll my clothes and stuff them into packing cubes by purpose and type. A whole square for activewear. I shove wool socks into shoes, underwear into open crevices. I leave what I don't need behind. A $7 sweater from Goodwill. A slightly oversized rain jacket. Half a burnt candle. You.

I wonder if this is how I've come to approach love: as ephemeral and inevitably ending. I share pieces of my heart and then close it up again. I write you out of my body with words I don't need anymore. When they ask about you, I pretend I'm not confused about why love never works. I shut my suitcase and zip it up. I leave what I don't need behind.

ROOT SPROUT

Driven away from damaged stems, adventitious root sprouts move to new areas that favor their growth and survival.

Places are visceral, like the smell of a lavender bush or a fresh pile of poop. *Ahorita* can mean five minutes or five hours from now. Andrea and I pass scissors back and forth to shape mesh and shade the plants from the scorching sun. Wiping our sweaty brows, we swap stories about maternal frustrations and toxic fathers. The budding arugula thanks us for our time, determined to grow like us, a Chilanga and Americana, both painfully aware of the shortness of good moments. At breakfast, she cures her headache with a fresh fist from the lavender bush.

I try to fall in love by making it and when it doesn't happen I wonder, what's wrong with me?

Words like "Mom" and "dead" have no weight in Spanish.

On the phone with my family, I hear the M&M bag crinkle as they joke about me coming back to the States and getting a real job, an adult job, because I'm an adult now. I resent how different I am from my family. I imagine sitting on the sofa next to my sister, rubbing her back, pulling a fistful of M&Ms out of the bag.

My heartstrings pull me back to my roots, where I'm from but don't belong. I'll be back for Christmas, I promise. But not much longer than that.

Sometimes I let emotions flood down my throat, thick, red, and sweet. My biological dad calls me for the second time this week and tells me again that Mom told lies about him. He swears a lot and laughs like me. Mom's not alive to fact check, so I take another swig. I'm tipsy again like my therapist warned me about. So this is what it's like to pretend.

To go along with something you know won't grow.

Six months later, I'm home early, picking up double shifts at the lobster house to make enough money to leave again. I spend three months back in Mexico, three months in France, three months in…

A job brings me to Berkeley, California, where the sun shines over 250 days out of the year. Life's not so bad here. I meet a woman named Jackie. She paints. I start imagining the possibilities of staying in one place.

I Named My Honda Rhonda

Even though the mechanic said not to
even though the odometer said, *don't go far*

When Rhonda's internal temperature reached
a hundred degrees in the flats of Indiana
I wondered for the four-thousandth time

Is this a fucking mistake? How far can you go
before a line of luck snaps?

Why do I always leave when things get easy?
What am I searching for? What if I don't find it?

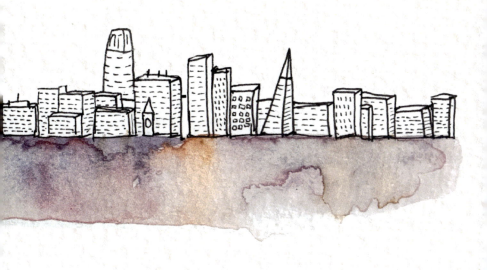

Rebloom

You long hair flippin' red lipstick wearing
chill girl

You boy whispering, laugh through the pain
put everyone first nice girl

You "no worries" sexual and assaulted
strong in all the quiet ways hot girl

Listen: one day
when you love yourself

You will make loud noises
and only laugh when it's funny

You'll seek time and space like a shadow seeks sun
use your voice like you never lost it

Shave your head and smirk your lips
say what you think because you think it

You'll wear your face raw with bare skin
take your problems off the back burner

And find yourself right at the corner
of hell yes and fuck no

Because not unlike an orchid,
you can and will rebloom

You Are Not Alone

From above, thousands of red lights stutter
Salt Lake City's inchoate rush hour

We left work early for once
caught the fingertips of the waning sun

And the mountains, lit from behind
effuse a gold, jack-o-lantern glow

A film sets over the basin
(actually, it's always there

We're just in it, so we never notice
oh, the living, how we trap ourselves)

The day arcs like a storyline
like the sun across the eternal sky

Even when smog envelopes the city
and a friend dies in his sleep at age thirty-two

And even when the steering wheel pulls you
down an old habit (I-111)

The sun perforates the cloud-smog and
radiates light in all directions

Including across our tight faces
where our dark under-eye bags disappear

Just for a second
a kaleidoscopic reminder

That you're not alone
your struggle is not only yours

That in life's living room
we all rise and retire with the sun

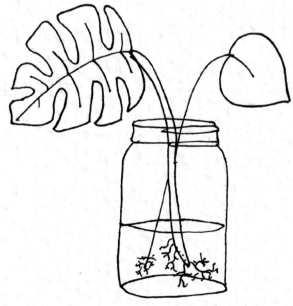

What to Remember on Hard Days

Feelings are like tunnels: you move through them
towards a light at the end
the meanest voice in your head can be replaced
with the nicest one
you are doing so well
you have come so far
there's no rush
mistakes are portals to growth and discovery
shame is just an emotion without a name: speak it
to release it
your mind is not always right
you are not alone
it's okay to slow down
profound action comes after profound rest
tomorrow is a new day
today is just a hard one

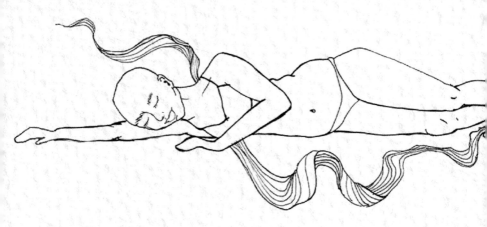

Don't Be Afraid of Your Silence

I stayed up
until Oakland went to bed and
I glimpsed

    the silence

It started as thoughts
my own voice filled the void that
the day crawled out of
ankles deep in my chaos
I remembered why I never liked

    the silence

But I took a breath
and another
until my mind stopped talking and I heard
the steady rhythm of my own body
a thrum that matched
the universe at rest
both of which continue without request
don't be afraid of

Or of the moments, unfilled
nothing scary lives there
you are always safe
with yourself

A Moose Told Me Not to Worry

I.
In the wooded grove
questions arise
like worms
in wet weather

The whys, hows,
whens, wheres, whos
litter, like wrappers,
the pineconed Earth

II.
With each wind-breath
the grand trees swell
your questions climb
their trunks

Nestle between
their swishing leaves
cozy up to the birds
call for their response

III.
With a gasp
you spot a moose
your questions meet
her sturdy gaze

She putters her
hooves to pause
from a hearty meal
in the wooded grove

IV.
She does not speak
in questions
she does not
question herself

She knows that
lost is always
on the way
to found

V.
A breeze weaves through
the stiffened silence and
the yearling
tilts her head

Your questions dissolve
into the evening mist
except for the important one
who are you?

VI.
The moose is not
pained by the question
she does not count
days in time lost

She mulls and munches
replete with ease
it's not obliviousness
it's just not worry

What to Do With Overwhelm

Overwhelm is
overdoing it
slow down
stop running
submit and surrender
ask the child inside
what she needs today
treasure her
it will be okay
at some point
you will feel better
you will look back and say
thank god
I took that time
to rest and replenish
to move through it
to nurture the child inside me
who was not loved
the way she needed to be
back then
you will be thankful
for leaning into it
for loving yourself

Something Is Changing Within Me

Something is changing within me:
I no longer worry about things I'm not doing
I spend Sundays in bed, writing my poems
I cuddle with coffee and the thoughts I'm pursuing

Something is changing within me:
I wear comfortable clothes and I let myself grow
I leave gatherings when I'm not feeling well
I don't always worry about things I don't know

Something is changing within me:
I'm not searching for something I can't seem to find
I'm not drinking my way through the parties
I'm starting to leave the old me behind

Something is changing within me:
I no longer want to be someone else
I'm grateful for all that I have right now
I wish I could tell my 16-year-old self

Woman in the Moonlight

Have you, of late,
gazed up at the sky
eyes caught by the Moon,
Her ecstasy awry?

Rounded She is,
as the seal's exposed head,
as the bellies of mothers,
revered in Her bed.

She goes and She comes,
with the flow of the tides,
emerging with poise,
behind cloud, She confides:

"O woman, be lit!
not scared or with woe,
if lost, then be found,
in My light, you will glow!"

ROOT SYSTEM

Root systems deliver nutrients, store energy from the sun, and anchor the plant to Earth. Healthy roots allow the plant to grow and thrive.

When I move in with Jackie under our first lease, my room starts bare to the bones: white walls, a lamp, and a bed, at least on a frame. I watch Jackie drive big, beautiful furniture over from her Mom's house. She puts two dressers and a hutch into her Mom's partner's pickup and loses pieces of them to the 5. It takes a gaggle of us to get them into the house. One by one, she marries plants and hangs paintings on the walls. She never over-clutters, never brings in junk, never lets it pile up, but always finds new corners of the house to bring to life.

In her footsteps, I paint my own pictures with a watercolor set she gives me for my birthday, and I hang them on my bare walls. I find an elegant Persian rug and buy it, despite the fear in my gut of owning something too heavy to carry and too valuable to throw away. And finally, I buy plants, the easy ones that grow even while you're away. The ones that welcome you home, weeks later, with new sprouts and longer roots.

The fear of rooting isn't completely gone. Sometimes, my closet gets too full, and I rip clothes off my hangers until I can picture each article by memory. Sometimes I worry about stagnation. I fear one day, I'll wake up surprised and unhappy with my life. But for now, I am trepidatiously filling my heart with our rooted moments: a daily cup of Jackie's strong-ass coffee, watching the pickiest plants thrive under her magic touch, feeling my creativity flow from the intention I pour into it. I can see how houses become havens. I'm learning to lay roots.

Woman in the Moonlight II

In power and trust,
the woman takes heed,
bathed by the Moon,
she begins her due bleed.

With every good ooze,
she finds her release,
womb cupped in her hand,
again the Moon speaks!

"Your truth is nay far,
within you, it rings,
once quiet, the noise,
your wisdom does sing."

There in Her light,
she closes her eyes,
listens, intent,
and to her surprise –

A voice like the Moon's
comes through in the clear!
could it be so?
was it always right here?

You Will Know What You Lived For

Think of the vignettes that will greet you when you're dying:
sitting in the morning sun and
that first sip of coffee
smelling rain before it starts
pizza before it's done
the cadence of your partner's giggle
when he pauses TV to say I love you
your first heartbreak
all the mountains you've climbed
the breeze that made you feel better
dinners with your chosen ones
eating mushrooms in the attic
your best friend's smile when she said we're forever
biking to class with the wind at your back
San Francisco lights
when Mom almost died
Berkeley's springtime florals
New Hampshire's snow whirls
the moments full of music
the ones that felt hopeless
car rides to new places
couch lounging with comfortable faces
the crinkling of skin
being a little afraid of
what comes at the end
they will play like a disjointed movie
you will know what they stand for
you will know what you lived for

Slanted Light

The steam from my coffee swirls into the air. It's raining for the first time in months — thank god. Each droplet chips away at the heatwave. My numbness splits open and spills onto the sidewalk. Neighbors in masks trickle out of their houses for a tickle of cool air; on morning runs, walking dogs, friends with coffees in hand. There's a calmness to their gait, the gift of Sundays.

I'm sitting on my porch — what a gift, this porch. The morning light shines in sideways. I just gave $2 to a man named Robert. It's his 53rd birthday today and his goal is to make $10. In these moments, I always debate whether to give $2 or $20. I usually give $2, even though I never find a good reason not to give $20. Oakland challenges me in ways that New Hampshire does not. I look at Robert's toothless grin and I wonder, why am I in this life and he in his? How do I have white skin and hot coffee and a porch with slanted light?

My Backyard in the Bay
(I'm not okay)

There's a sliver of concrete before the clovers begin where I put two camping chairs and a Home Depot bucket. Staying put is a slow accumulation of nicer things. I sit down next to no one and set my coffee on Home Depot. I look out onto the clovers, all their bright yellow projects folded and facing what they know to be the afternoon sun, the brightest part of the day. They'll wait for it.

Atop the roar of I-80 to San Francisco, the gulls caw and the warblers warb. The crocosmia pop through the understory and uncoil their goods for the hummingbird, who flashes her shimmery green bod to suck their juices. She gives way to the raised garden the renters left desolate with concrete chunks and broken porcelain, extremities of hollow wood from plants of days past.

The truth is, I came out here because I saw the sun slant through my bedroom window and wondered, will that make me feel better? I haven't been okay lately. I've been afraid before bed again. I'm missing Mom and motherly advice; seasons add up and feel like another life.

The wetness of winter in Oakland surprises my cheeks. These chairs hold my weight, this bucket holds my coffee, and the clover flowers hold my hurt, heads closed and bowed through the night, twisted remnants of something open and bright. The hummingbird holds the record for things done the

fastest, so I don't have to try. The warblers
return on cue, my loyal friends.
In the raised garden, I see hope. I
see porcelain-boarded rosemaries
and a budding lemon tree.
Two baby magueys — they'll be
giant, one day. I can be anything
I need to be. The truth is, I'm
feeling a little better.

You Can Enjoy the View

You can wake up and
drink all the warm liquids you want
you can buy a comfy new sweater and wear it with no shirt
or bra
you can read a poem instead of the news
you can go to the corner of your mind where the worries
don't live
you can forgive yourself for
killing your monstera
you can let your guard down
with the good ones
you can go outside for sunset and
bathe in pink and yellow
you can walk slower when you're tired
you can eat when you're hungry
you can lay roots
you can dance
you can play
you can stay
you can be safe
you can enjoy the view

Laying Roots

I signed my first lease and bought a fern
its green fronds bounced at every turn
alongside the habits I sought to unlearn

I loved it so much, I ripped it in half
so I could have more and prove to myself
that broken things can grow themselves back

Its long leaves crisped up, folded, curled under
stopped growing at all and left me to wonder
will the parts that are dead ever recover?

I put the plant in a sunlit corner
dressed in the armor of an explorer
left on a trip to a place that was warmer

Upon my return, the fern had a sprout!
so cute, so green, with the same little bounce
somehow it grew, despite all my doubts

Fragile, but ready, it said it would try
I promised it patience and the blessing of time
roots aren't always easy to come by

As my fern started over, I realized my hurt
adventitious roots are born from high alert
I found out my fern and I share the same dirt

The Healing Process

You worry what happens with nowhere to run,
you can't help the feeling of coming undone,
the thrill of it all can no longer assuage,
your traumatized heart and the chaos of change.

You book a one-way to a good, heartfelt place,
you start to enjoy its unusual pace,
nothing strikes you wrong about a friendly face,
with an experienced gait your nerves are replaced.

You sit with silence and the noise that guards it,
you nav to the store without Google to mark it,
you buy plants, good knives, and all the bulk spice,
you allow yourself comfort and things that are nice.

Growing a Garden

I used to dream of faraway places,
rolling green pastures and wide-open spaces.

I imagined just how big I could grow,
with no one to tell me what roots I should sow.

For years on adventures, I went far and wide,
exchanged smiles with strangers and beds by the night.

Away from the hurt of my childhood house,
I sprouted brand new parts of myself.

Yet, after a while, it wore on my soul,
no matter how hard I tried, I couldn't feel whole.

That's what it took to come off the road:
the hug of two friends and the promise of home.

I started to dream of places nearby,
the same trusted faces, a good, stable life.

I got bedsheets and plants, my grandmother's dishes,
put my suitcase away and had my first Christmas.

Sometimes it takes special people to root,
plants form a garden with more than just two.

Dead Sunflower Sprouts

Sunflowers remind me of you, Mom,
because you had them everywhere
hanging on walls (live laugh love)
painted on mugs
growing by the patio

But if you were alive
it would not be my favorite flower
and I would not have it tattooed across my ribs
if you were alive
I would not have swerved my car
into the breakdown lane
to pick one off the side of the highway

(Only to discover
it was not a sunflower
it was just an enlarged daisy or something)

My roommate gave me sunflower seeds to grow
and I killed the sprouts and wondered
is this just another way I lose you
like I lost your voice and your laugh?
is there a way something dead grows itself back?

Sunflowers remind me of you, Mom,
but even though I killed them
I can still find you in the humor
of trying to grow a sunflower
in a dark room
when all it needed
was a little sun

What You Can Do With Your Darkness

Perhaps you will be born
not once but over and over
because what is birth
other than entering a world unknown
brilliant and harsh
like jumping off a dock
into the lake's chilly abyss.

Perhaps you will learn
not just from the creased hand of an aged person
but on your own and forever
because what is learning
other than discovering the existence of things
that butterflies start in a crawl, too
that all things marvelous are somehow fragile.

Perhaps you will dream
not only at night but with eyes wide open
of things truly imaginable
because what is dreaming
other than knowing yourself
like the back of your hand and
writing that verity into life's rocky gait.

Perhaps you will love
not only others but yourself
because what is love
other than shining a light
into the deepest crevices of your being
and realizing that without that darkness
you'd never see the moon.

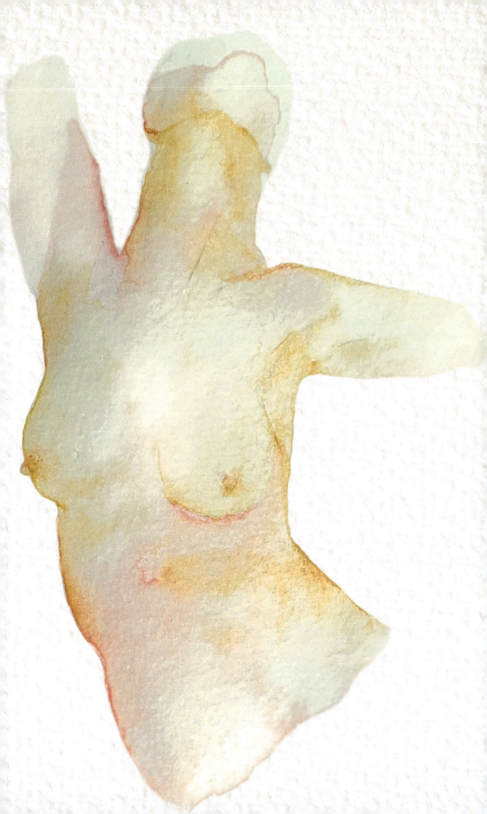

About the Author
AMANDA SPILLER

Amanda Spiller is an artist and adventurer. As a survivor of childhood trauma and the early loss of her mother, she uses words to explore grief and healing.

Amanda has helped countless artists and multimillion-dollar brands tell their stories. But lately, she's telling her own.

About the Illustrator
JACKIE ZINTEL

Jackie Zintel is a Bay Area creator, cyclist, and prevailing optimist, no matter what life brings. She lived from a suitcase for many years before getting a cat and settling into stillness.

Jackie is excited to pour love into life and see what blooms.

Gratitude

Thanks, Mom, for molding me resilient before you died.

Thank you to my beautiful illustrator Jackie for holding this project in your heart and bringing it to life with your hands.

To my editors and designers Brennan DeFrisco, Allie Marini, Sara Shopkow, and Marisa Randles: every poet needs you. Thank you for creating safe spaces. Thank you for believing in me. Thank you for being excited about this book.

Thank you, family: Dad, Ben, Julia, and the extended Spillers, for your potent love and patience.

To my sister Sara, thanks for being there through it all, helping me survive, and giving me strength when I had none.

To my girls Chrissy, Kelsey, Christina, and Amanda, thanks for loving me at my best and my worst.

To Elle, you are the sun to my flower. Thank you for your endless light and support.

Thank you, Luigi, for feeding my mouth and my soul at the same time.

To Mary Oliver, Suleika Jaouad, Raisa Tolchinsky, Esmé Wang, Yung Pueblo, Olivia Gatwood,

Adrienne Rich, Susan Faludi, Cheryl Strayed: thanks for showing me the way.

Acknowledgments

"My Backyard in the Bay (I'm not okay)" first seen in *Quiet Lightning*'s literary mixtape, 2021.

"What You Can Do With Darkness" first seen in *The Moving Force Journal* as "The Journey," 2019.

"Woman in the Moonlight I" first seen in *SIREN Magazine*, 2018.

Stay in touch!

Visit amandaspiller.com or
send your thoughts to amanda@amandaspiller.com